Introduction

Combine simple embroidery stitches, red embroidery floss and red and white fabrics, and soon you will have created the sweet designs shown on the following pages.

Whether you start with the table runner and place mats or any of the other projects, your home will be filled with whimsical garden projects.

The redwork designs shown in this book can be used for many other projects as well. Simply choose the design and trace it on a white or cream fabric. Then add it to any item of your choice, such as clothing, bags, pillows, pillowcases, etc., to make a creative work of your own.

Hand stitching is a wonderful way to relax the body and soul. Creating fun and functional redwork embroidery projects will bring you hours of fulfilling enjoyment. You'll love making these unique projects to add a special touch to your home and as gifts for others. ❖

Meet the Designer

I simply love to design projects that make people smile. Even as a small child, I enjoyed making things out of paper, clay and fabric.

As a young mother of three sons and wife of a very busy husband, I wanted to make additional money for all of the extras every family needs. One of the earliest businesses I created was a Barbie® doll party. I would have my friends and their moms hold a Barbie doll party, and I would show a collection of doll clothes that I had designed. They would order what they wanted, and I would then deliver and charge for the wardrobes that had been ordered. It was a great learning experience.

In 1989, I started the Pearl Louise Designs pattern company and started showing my designs at the International Quilt Market. When my local quilt shop closed, I decided to open The Thimble Cottage Quilt Village quilt shop. This move enabled me to have quilt-shop fabrics at my fingertips. The quilt shop and my home are in Rapid City, S.D., just a few miles from Mount Rushmore. During the summer months, we are very busy with customers from all over the world. I truly enjoy visiting with all of them.

Over the years, the shop has evolved into a place where customers can come and enjoy our collections of fabrics, classes and clubs that we offer. In addition, we have a Web store (www.thimblecottage.com).

I began designing fabric for the Troy Corporation several years ago and have found it very interesting and challenging. Most of my designs are whimsical with a home-decorating flair that adds tons of fun when designing.

My husband, Fred, and I enjoy fishing in the summer months. We have three grown sons, darling daughters-in-law and three wonderful grandchildren. Bella and Kate, our dogs, travel with us, and Bella goes to the quilt shop with me every day.

One of my favorite sayings is "Happiness is homemade," and I am happy all the time. I hope you will be too! ❖

Redwork Basics

Redwork embroidery requires a few supplies and some simple instructions. Read through these basics before you select and begin stitching one of the whimsical projects in this book.

Supplies

Fabric

Use good-quality, 100 percent cotton fabrics in your redwork quilts or projects. The projects in this book were made using white and cream tonals, but any white, off-white or cream high-quality cotton fabric can be used.

Pre-washing your fabrics is recommended, but not absolutely necessary. If you choose not to pre-wash, you must test the fabrics to make sure that they are colorfast and won't shrink.

Start by cutting a 2" by fabric width strip of each fabric you have selected for your redwork project; measure and record the width of each strip.

To determine whether the fabric is colorfast, immerse each strip separately into a clean bowl of extremely hot water or hold the fabric strip under hot running water. If your fabric bleeds a great deal, all is not necessarily lost. You might be able to wash all of that fabric until all of the excess dye has washed out. Fabrics that continue to bleed after they have been washed several times should be eliminated. You do not want the red fabrics bleeding onto the embroidered squares.

To test for shrinkage, iron each saturated strip dry with a hot iron. When the strip is completely dry, measure and compare the size to the original recorded length. If all of your fabric strips shrink about the same amount, then you have no problem. When you wash your finished quilt or project, you may achieve the puckered look of an antique quilt. If you do not want this look, you will have to wash and dry all fabrics before beginning so that shrinkage is no longer a problem. If one of the fabrics shrinks more than the others, it should be eliminated.

Needles

There are several different types and sizes of needles that can be used for embroidery, Sharps— sizes 7–10—and embroidery needles—sizes 7 and 8 with a longer needle eye for easier threading—are popular. You should choose the size and type of needle you are comfortable with to do your embroidery.

Embroidery Floss

Six-strand cotton embroidery floss was used to embroider the designs in these redwork projects. Work with 1 strand in 18" lengths. You may choose to use two strands if you like, especially to stitch the designs on the towels. For the redwork, choose a shade of red such as Anchor 1005 or DMC 498. Be sure the floss you use is guaranteed to be colorfast.

Embroidery Hoops

The best embroidery results are achieved when using an embroidery hoop to hold the fabric taut while stitching. There are several types and sizes of hoops available on the market. Wooden hoops with an adjustable screw are the most common, but there are also spring hoops and the newer Q-snaps. Use the type and size hoop you find most comfortable for embroidering. If possible, it is best to use a hoop that is larger than the design you are embroidering. This helps you avoid having the hoop distort stitches when moved to other areas.

Redwork Embroidery

Tracing the Design

Cut fabric to be embroidered into the size specified with each project's instructions.

Center fabric over the printed design and trace using a sharp lead pencil or fabric marking pen or pencil. If you use a fabric pen, be sure to follow the manufacturer's directions for proper use. If you cannot see the lines clearly, use a light box for tracing. Remember that the tracing lines should not be visible on the finished project.

Embroidering the Design

Wash your hands before you start hand embroidery to avoid soiling the fabric. Thread floss into needle; do not tie a knot in end.

To begin stitching, come up from the wrong side of the fabric, leaving a 1" tail on the wrong side. Hold the floss end in place so that it is overcast with the first few stitches that are made. Cut the excess floss close to your work when finished.

Another way to begin stitching is to weave floss through several stitches on the wrong side of your work first.

As you embroider separate lines in a close area, it is best to carry the floss across the back as long as the distance is not more than 1". If the lines are more than 1" apart, weave the floss through a few stitches on the back side.

Never carry floss across an unworked area. The floss will show through on the finished project.

When finished stitching, weave floss through several stitches on the back side and cut away excess floss.

The Stitches

The stem stitch is the main stitch used to outline redwork designs. To execute the stem stitch, bring the needle up at position A (Figure 1). Hold floss down with the thumb of your non-stitching hand. Reinsert the needle at B and bring up at C, about halfway between A and B. Pull the floss through and continue in this manner with floss held below stitching line and working from left to right.

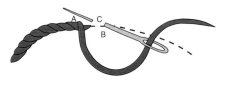

Figure 1

The backstitch may be used to cover right curves and can also be used to outline the designs if desired.

To execute the backstitch, bring needle up at A (Figure 2), a stitch length away from the beginning of the design line. Stitch back down at B at the beginning of the line, bring needle up at C and then stitch back down to meet previous stitch at A. Continue in this manner, working in a right-to-left direction.

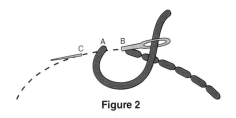

Figure 2

House of White Birches, Berne, Indiana 46711   Clotilde.com

The straight stitch (Figure 3) was used to cover small, straight lines. Come up at A and down at B. Straight stitches can be done in varying sizes and spaced regularly or irregularly.

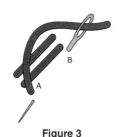

Figure 3

French knots (Figure 4) were used for eyes and any other place where a small dot was needed. Bring needle up at A. Wrap floss once around shaft of needle. Insert point of needle at B (close to, but not into A). Hold knot down as you pull needle through to back of fabric.

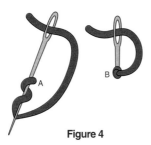

Figure 4

The Lazy Daisy (Figure 5) stitch was used for several of the flowers in the projects. Bring the needle up in the flower center and hold the floss with your left thumb. Insert the needle back into fabric where it first came out. Take the needle through the fabric, moving the point of the needle out a short distance away. Wrap the floss under the point of the needle and pull the needle back through the fabric. Secure the loop with a small stitch to finish one petal.

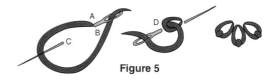

Figure 5

Finishing the Embroidered Block

When embroidery is completed, you may wash in cool water if soiled. To press, place block facedown on a hard, padded surface (ironing board with terry towel works fine); press carefully.

Trim block to measurement specified in individual project instructions, being sure to center the design. To do this, find the approximate center of the design and measure an equal distance to all four sides. For example, if the block is to be cut at 6½" x 6½", measure 3¼" from the center point to each side and trim. A wide acrylic ruler and a rotary cutter will aid in measuring and cutting. ❖

Good Morning Sunshine Wall Quilt

Add a touch of redwork sunshine to any room in your home with this embroidered project.

Project Specifications
Skill Level: Beginner
Quilt Size: 18" x 10" without prairie points
Block Size: 16" x 8"
Number of Blocks: 1

Good Morning Sunshine
16" x 8" Block
Make 1

Materials
- 1 fat quarter
  red print
- ⅝ yard white tonal
- Batting 18½" x 10½"
- Backing 18½" x 10½"
- All-purpose thread to match fabrics
- White quilting thread
- Red embroidery floss
- Large-eye embroidery needle
- Basic sewing tools and supplies

Cutting
1. Cut one 18" by fabric width strip white tonal; subcut strip into one 10" A rectangle.

2. Subcut the remainder of the strip cut in step 1 into four 2½"-wide strips; subcut these strips into (28) 2½" D squares.

3. Cut two 1½" x 16½" B strips red print.

4. Cut one 1½" x 21" strip red print; subcut strip into two 10½" C strips.

5. Cut three 2½" x 21" strips red print; subcut strips into (24) 2½" E squares.

Completing the Embroidered Block

1. Fold and crease the A rectangle to mark the vertical and horizontal centers.

2. Center and transfer the Good Morning Sunshine embroidery design on pages 8–9 to the A rectangle referring to Redwork Basics on page 2.

3. Complete the redwork embroidery on the marked rectangle referring to Redwork Basics on page 2.

4. Trim the embroidered A rectangle to 16½" x 8½", centering the design, to complete the Good Morning Sunshine block.

Completing the Wall Quilt

1. Sew B strips to opposite long sides and C strips to each short side of the Good Morning Sunshine block to complete the quilt top; press seams toward B and C strips.

2. Fold each D and E square in half on one diagonal with wrong sides together; fold in half again and press as shown in Figure 1.

Figure 1

3. Select five folded D triangles and pin to one C side of the quilted top matching raw edges and overlapping ends to make fit as shown in Figure 2; machine-baste to hold in place. *Note: The open ends all face in the same direction.*

Figure 2   **Figure 3**

4. Select four folded E triangles and pin between the D triangles as shown in Figure 3; machine-baste to hold in place.

5. Repeat steps 3 and 4 on the opposite C side of the quilted pillow top.

6. Repeat step 3 on the B sides of the wall quilt with nine D triangles and step 4 with eight folded E triangles as shown in Figure 4.

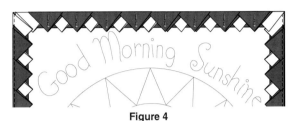

Figure 4

7. Press the pieced top on both sides; check for proper seam pressing and trim all loose threads.

8. Place the batting on a flat surface with the backing piece right side up on top; place the completed top right sides together with the backing with the prairie points between the layers; stitch all around, leaving a 5" opening on one side.

9. Trim batting close to seams; clip corners. Turn right side out through the opening and press edges flat; pin layers together to hold.

10. Hand-stitch opening edges closed.

11. Quilt as desired by hand or machine to complete the wall quilt. *Note: The sample wall quilt was machine-quilted in a meandering design using white thread.* ❖

Good Morning Sunshine Wall Quilt
Placement Diagram 18" x 10"
without prairie points

8

A

Place line on fold to make complete pattern

B

Garden Party Stitchery

Place line on fold to make complete pattern

A

B

House of White Birches, Berne, Indiana 46711   Clotilde.com

Good Morning Sunshine Pillow

Consider this cheerful pillow your wake-up call—
or an invitation to snooze just a minute more!

Project Specifications
Skill Level: Beginner
Pillow Size: 18" x 10" without prairie points
Block Size: 16" x 8"

Good Morning Sunshine
16" x 8" Block
Make 1

Materials
- ⅝ yard red print
- ⅝ yard white tonal
- Batting 26" x 18"
- Backing 26" x 18"
- All-purpose thread to match fabrics
- White quilting thread
- Red embroidery floss
- Large-eye embroidery needle
- Polyester fiberfill
- Basic sewing tools and supplies

Cutting
1. Cut one 18" by fabric width strip white tonal; subcut strip into one 10" A rectangle.

2. Subcut the remainder of the strip cut in step 1 into four 2½"-wide strips; subcut these strips into (30) 2½" D squares.

3. Cut one 18½" by fabric width strip red print; subcut strip into one 10½" rectangle for pillow back. Subcut the remainder of the strip into three 2½"-wide strips and three 1½"-wide strips.

4. Subcut the 1½"-wide strips into two 16½" B strips and two 10½" C strips.

5. Subcut the 2½"-wide strips into a total of (26) 2½" E squares.

Completing the Embroidered Block
1. Fold and crease the A rectangle to mark the vertical and horizontal centers.

2. Center and transfer the Good Morning Sunshine embroidery design on pages 8–9 to the A rectangle referring to Redwork Basics on page 2.

3. Complete the redwork embroidery on the marked rectangle referring to Redwork Basics on page 2.

4. Trim the embroidered A rectangle to 16½" x 8½", centering the design, to complete the Good Morning Sunshine block.

Completing the Pillow
1. Sew B strips to opposite long sides and C strips to each short side of the Good Morning Sunshine block to complete the pillow top; press seams toward B and C strips.

2. Press the pieced top on both sides; check for proper seam pressing and trim all loose threads.

3. Sandwich the batting rectangle between the completed top and the prepared backing piece; pin or baste layers together to hold. Quilt as desired by hand or machine. *Note: The sample pillow was machine-quilted in a meandering design using white thread.*

4. When quilting is complete, trim batting and backing fabric even with raw edges of the pillow top.

5. Fold each D and E square in half on one diagonal with wrong sides together; fold in half again and press as shown in Figure 1.

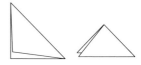

Figure 1

6. Select five folded D triangles and pin to one C side of the quilted pillow top matching raw edges and overlapping ends to make fit as shown in Figure 2; machine-baste to hold in place. *Note: The open ends all face in the same direction.*

7. Select four folded E triangles and pin between the D triangles as shown in Figure 3; machine-baste to hold in place.

8. Repeat steps 6 and 7 on the opposite C side of the quilted pillow top.

9. Repeat step 6 on the B sides of the pillow top with 10 D triangles and step 7 with nine folded E triangles as shown in Figure 4.

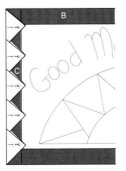

Figure 2

Figure 3

Figure 4

House of White Birches, Berne, Indiana 46711 Clotilde.com

10. Place the red print pillow back right sides together with the quilted top with the prairie points between the layers; stitch all around, leaving a 5" opening on one side.

11. Turn right side out through the opening; poke out corners and press flat.

12. Insert polyester fiberfill stuffing to desired fullness.

13. Hand-stitch the opening closed to complete the pillow. ❖

Good Morning Sunshine Pillow
Placement Diagram 18" x 10" without prairie points

Garden Party Sampler

No matter the weather, this wall quilt will bring a touch of spring or summer sunshine to any room. The easy-to-stitch embroidery designs and pieced border add a touch of cottage charm to this whimsical wall quilt.

Project Specifications
Skill Level: Intermediate
Quilt Size: 36" x 44"
Block Sizes: 6" x 6", 12" x 14" and 14" x 4"
Number of Blocks: 14, 1 and 1

Materials
- 6 fat quarters assorted white/cream tonals
- 7 fat quarters assorted red/burgundy prints/tonals/mottleds
- ½ yard burgundy mottled
- Batting 44" x 52"
- Backing 44" x 52"
- All-purpose thread to match fabrics
- Red and cream quilting thread
- Red embroidery floss
- Large-eye embroidery needle
- Basic sewing tools and supplies

Cutting
1. Cut three 1½" x 21" strips from each of the red/burgundy fabrics; subcut these strips into 14 matching pairs of 6½" E strips and 14 matching pairs of 8½" F strips.

2. Cut a total of two 1½" x 4½" G strips and two 1½" x 16½" H strips from the red/burgundy fabrics.

3. Cut a total of (30) 3¼" x 3¼" D squares from the red/burgundy fabrics.

4. Cut a total of (36) 2½" x 4½" I rectangles and four 2½" x 2½" K squares red/burgundy fabrics for outer border units.

5. Cut (72) 2½" x 2½" J squares white/cream tonals.

6. Cut a total of (14) 7½" x 7½" B squares white/cream tonals.

7. Cut one 13" x 15" A rectangle white/cream tonal.

8. Cut one 15" x 5" C rectangle white/cream tonal.

9. Cut five 2¼" by fabric width strips burgundy mottled for binding.

House of White Birches, Berne, Indiana 46711 Clotilde.com

14

Completing the Embroidered Blocks

1. Fold and crease each A and C rectangle and B square to mark the vertical and horizontal centers.

2. Center and transfer the smaller designs to the B squares, the Bird & Blossoms design to the C rectangle and the Garden Club design to the A rectangle referring to Redwork Basics on page 2.

3. Complete the redwork embroidery on all marked squares and rectangles referring to Redwork Basics on page 2.

4. Trim the embroidered B squares to 6½" x 6½", centering the designs, to complete the blocks.

5. Trim the embroidered A rectangle to 12½" x 14½", centering the design, to complete the Garden Club block.

6. Trim the embroidered C rectangle to 14½" x 4½", centering the design, to complete the Bird & Blossoms block.

Completing the Pieced Center

1. Draw a diagonal line from corner to corner on the wrong side of half of the D squares.

2. Place a marked D square and different fabric unmarked D square right sides together and sew a ¼" seam on each side of the marked line as shown in Figure 1.

Figure 1

3. Cut the stitched unit apart on the marked line to make two D units as shown in Figure 2; press the units open with seam to one side.

Figure 2

4. Repeat steps 2 and 3 with the remaining D squares to make a total of 30 D units.

5. Divide the D units in half and draw a diagonal line from corner to corner on the wrong side of half of the units referring to Figure 3.

Figure 3

6. Place a marked D unit right sides together with an unmarked different fabric D unit and stitch ¼" on each side of the marked line as shown in Figure 4.

Figure 4

7. Cut the stitched D units apart to make two D-D units as shown in Figure 5; press seam to one side.

Figure 5

8. Repeat steps 6 and 7 to complete a total of 30 D-D units.

9. Select and join six D-D units to make a strip as shown in Figure 6; press seams in one direction. Repeat to make a second strip.

Figure 6

10. Sew a pieced strip to the top and bottom of the Garden Club block (A); press seams away from the pieced strip.

11. Select and join nine D-D units to make a strip as shown in Figure 7; press seams in one direction. Repeat to make a second strip.

Figure 7

12. Sew a pieced strip to opposite long sides of the Garden Club block (A); press seams away from the pieced strips.

13. Sew a G strip to opposite short ends and H strips to the top and bottom of the embroidered Bird & Blossoms block (C) as shown in Figure 8; press seams toward G and H strips.

Figure 8

14. Sew the bordered Bird & Blossoms block to the bottom of the bordered Garden Club block to complete the pieced center as shown in Figure 9.

Figure 9

Completing the Pieced Top

1. Divide the embroidered B squares into two piles as follows: Pile 1—Watering Can, Flower Pot, Garden Gate, Garden Bonnet, Heart Blossom, Honey Blossoms and Garden Glove. Pile 2—Blossom Row, Garden Tools, Home Sweet Home, Summer Bird Song, Blossom Basket, Garden Cart and Butterfly Garden.

2. Select one of the Pile 1 blocks and two matching E strips and two matching F strips.

3. Sew an E strip to the top and bottom and F to opposite sides of the Pile 1 block as shown in Figure 10; press seams toward E and F strips.

Figure 10

4. Repeat steps 2 and 3 with all Pile 1 blocks.

5. Select one of the Pile 2 blocks and two matching E strips and two matching F strips.

6. Sew an E strip to opposite sides and F strips to the top and bottom of the Pile 2 block as shown in Figure 11; press seams toward E and F strips.

Figure 11

7. Repeat steps 5 and 6 with all Pile 2 blocks.

8. Select and join the Home Sweet Home and Flower Pot blocks to make the top row as shown in Figure 12; press seam to one side.

Figure 12

9. Sew this row to the top of the pieced center; press seam toward the row.

10. Select and join the Garden Tools and Watering Can blocks to make the bottom row as shown in Figure 13; press seam to one side.

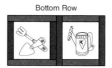

Figure 13

11. Sew this row to the bottom of the pieced center; press seam toward the row.

12. Select and join the Garden Gate, Garden Cart, Heart Blossom, Summer Bird Song and Garden Glove blocks to make the left-side row as shown in Figure 14; press seams in one direction.

Figure 14

13. Sew this row to the left-side edge of the pieced center; press seam toward the row.

14. Select and join the Butterfly Garden, Garden Bonnet, Blossom Basket, Honey Blossoms and Blossom Row blocks to make the right-side row, again referring to Figure 14.

15. Draw a diagonal line from corner to corner on the wrong side of each J square.

16. Place a marked J square right sides together on one end of an I rectangle and stitch on the marked line as shown in Figure 15; trim seam to ¼" and press J to the right side, again referring to Figure 15.

Figure 15

17. Place a second marked J square on the opposite end of the stitched unit and repeat step 16 to complete one I-J unit referring to Figure 16.

Figure 16

18. Repeat steps 16 and 17 to complete a total of 36 I-J units.

19. Select and join 10 I-J units to make a side border strip; press seams in one direction. Repeat to make a second side border strip.

20. Sew a side border strip to opposite long sides of the pieced center referring to the Placement Diagram for positioning of the pieced strips; press seams away from the pieced strips.

21. Select and join eight I-J units to make the top border strip; sew a K square to each end of the strip. Press seams in one direction and toward K. Repeat to make the bottom border strip.

22. Sew the pieced strips to the top and bottom of the pieced center; press seams away from the pieced strips to complete the pieced top.

Finishing

1. Press quilt top on both sides; check for proper seam pressing and trim all loose threads.

2. Sandwich batting between the stitched top and the backing piece; pin or baste layers together to hold. Quilt as desired by hand or machine. *Note: The sample quilt was machine-quilted in a meandering*

design using cream thread in the cream pieces and red thread in the red/burgundy pieces.

3. When quilting is complete, trim batting and backing fabric even with raw edges of quilt top.

4. Join binding strips on short ends with diagonal seams to make one long strip as shown in Figure 17; trim seams to ¼" and press seams open.

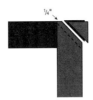

Figure 17

5. Fold the binding strip with wrong sides together along length; press.

6. Sew binding to quilt edges, mitering corners and overlapping ends. Fold binding to the back side and stitch in place to finish. ❖

Garden Party Sampler
Placement Diagram 36" x 44"

18

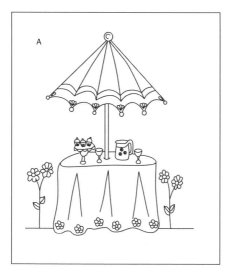

Garden Club
12" x 14"Block
Make 1

Bird & Blossoms
14" x 4" Block
Make 1

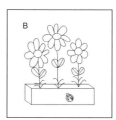

Home Sweet Home
6" x 6" Block
Make 1

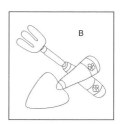

Garden Tools
6" x 6" Block
Make 1

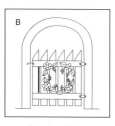

Garden Gate
6" x 6" Block
Make 1

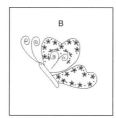

Butterfly Garden
6" x 6" Block
Make 1

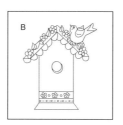

Summer Bird Song
6" x 6" Block
Make 1

Blossom Row
6" x 6" Block
Make 1

Garden Cart
6" x 6" Block
Make 1

Heart Blossom
6" x 6" Block
Make 1

Watering Can
6" x 6" Block
Make 1

Garden Glove
6" x 6" Block
Make 1

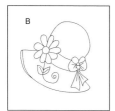

Garden Bonnet
6" x 6" Block
Make 1

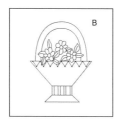

Blossom Basket
6" x 6" Block
Make 1

Honey Blossoms
6" x 6" Block
Make 1

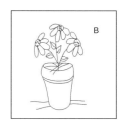

Flower Pot
6" x 6" Block
Make 1

Blossom Basket Embroidery Design

Bird & Blossoms Embroidery Design

Butterfly Garden Embroidery Design

Blossom Row Embroidery Design

Garden Bonnet Embroidery Design

Flower Pot Embroidery Design

Garden Cart Embroidery Design

House of White Birches, Berne, Indiana 46711   Clotilde.com

Match on line to make complete pattern

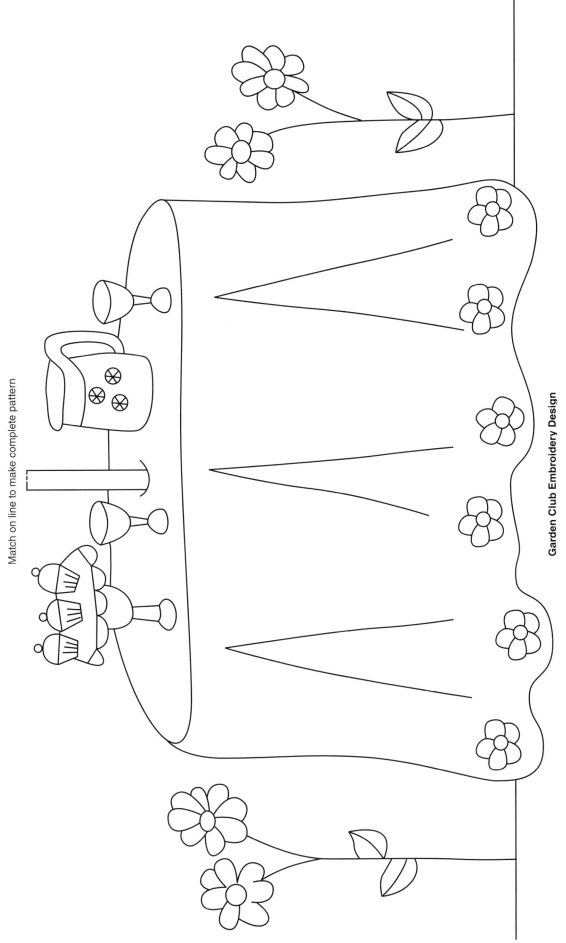

Match on line to make complete pattern

Garden Club Embroidery Design

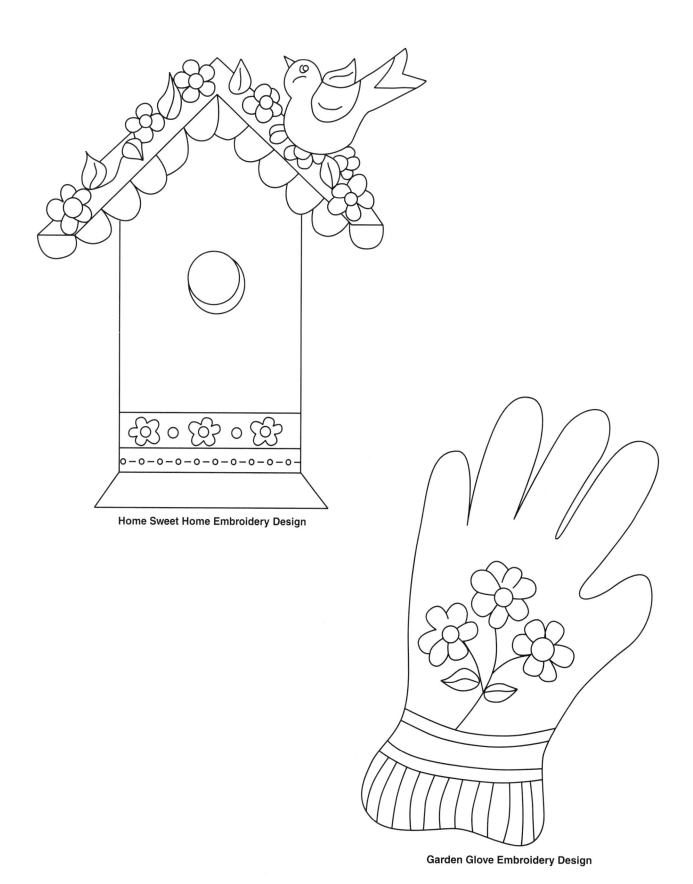

Home Sweet Home Embroidery Design

Garden Glove Embroidery Design

Summer Bird Song Embroidery Design

Garden Gate Embroidery Design

House of White Birches, Berne, Indiana 46711   Clotilde.com

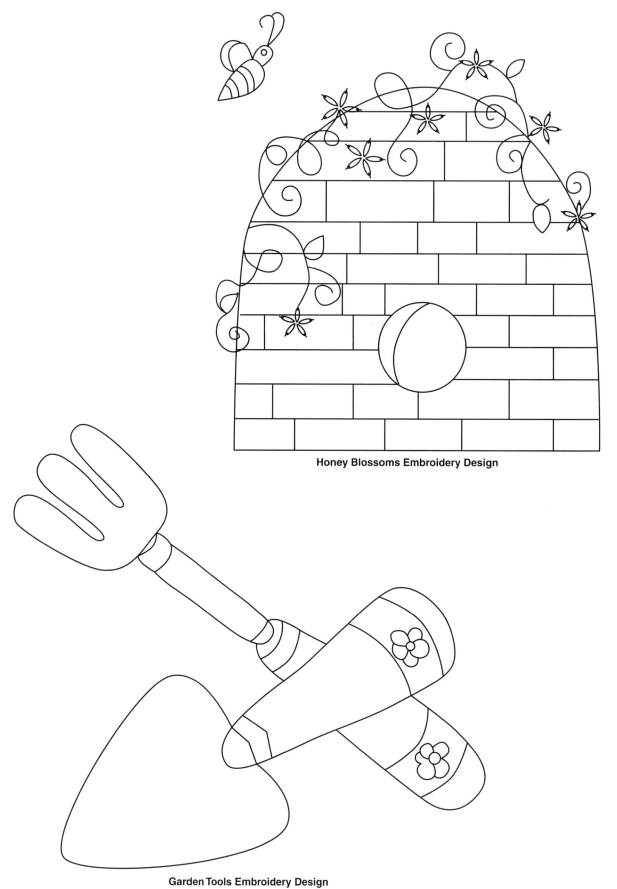

Honey Blossoms Embroidery Design

Garden Tools Embroidery Design

Heart Blossom Embroidery Design

Watering Can Embroidery Design

Floral Bouquet Wall Quilt

Embroider this everlasting redwork bouquet to decorate any room in your home.

Project Specifications
Skill Level: Beginner
Wall Quilt Size: 14" x 22"
Block Size: 8" x 16"
Number of Blocks: 1

Materials
- 2 (1½" x 22½") G strips burgundy tonal
- 2 (1½" x 10½") C strips red/burgundy tonal
- ⅓ yard red tonal
- ⅝ yard white/cream tonal
- Batting 22" x 30"
- Backing 22" x 30"
- All-purpose thread to match fabrics
- Red and white quilting thread
- Red embroidery floss
- Large-eye embroidery needle
- Basic sewing tools and supplies

Floral Bouquet
8" x 18" Block
Make 1

Cutting
1. Cut one 18" by fabric width strip white/cream tonal; subcut strip into one 10" A rectangle. Trim the remainder of the strip into two 1½" x 10½" D strips and two 1½" x 20½" E strips.

2. Cut two 1½" by fabric width strips red tonal; subcut strips into two 16½" B strips and two 12½" F strips.

3. Cut two 2¼" by fabric width strips red tonal for binding.

Completing the Embroidered Blocks
1. Fold and crease the A rectangle to mark the vertical and horizontal centers.

2. Center and transfer the Floral Bouquet embroidery design to the A rectangle referring to Redwork Basics on page 2.

3. Complete the redwork embroidery on the marked rectangle referring to Redwork Basics on page 2.

4. Trim the embroidered A rectangle to 8½" x 16½", centering the design, to complete the Floral Bouquet design.

Completing the Wall Quilt
1. Sew a B strip to opposite long sides and C strips to the top and bottom of the Floral Bouquet block; press seams toward B and C strips.

2. Sew D strips to the top and bottom and E strips to opposite sides of the bordered block; press seams toward D and E strips.

3. Sew F strips to the top and bottom and G strips to opposite long sides of the bordered block; press seams toward the F and G strips to complete the pieced top.

4. Press the pieced top on both sides; check for proper seam pressing and trim all loose threads.

5. Sandwich the batting rectangle between the completed top and the prepared backing piece; pin or baste layers together to hold. Quilt as desired by hand or machine. *Note: The sample wall quilt was machine-quilted in a meandering design using cream thread in the cream pieces and red thread in the red/burgundy pieces.*

6. When quilting is complete, trim batting and backing fabric even with raw edges of the quilt top.

7. Join binding strips on short ends with diagonal seams to make one long strip as shown in Figure 1; trim seams to ¼" and press seams open.

Figure1

8. Fold the binding strip with wrong sides together along length; press.

9. Sew binding to the wall quilt edges, mitering corners and overlapping ends. Fold binding to the back side and stitch in place to finish the wall quilt. ❖

Floral Bouquet
Placement Diagram 14" x 22"

Match on
line to make
complete design

Match on
line to make
complete design

House of White Birches, Berne, Indiana 46711   Clotilde.com

Bouquet in a Jar Place Mats

These place mats will look great on any table by themselves or with the Bouquet in a Jar Table Runner.

Project Specifications
Skill Level: Beginner
Place Mat Size: 18" x 12"
Block Size: 6" x 10"
Number of Blocks: 2

Materials
- 1 fat quarter dark red/burgundy mottled
- 1 fat quarter medium red/burgundy tonal
- ⅝ yard burgundy mottled
- 1⅛ yards white/cream tonal
- 2 rectangles batting 22" x 16"
- All-purpose thread to match fabrics
- Red and white quilting thread
- Red embroidery floss
- Large-eye embroidery needle
- Basic sewing tools and supplies

Cutting
Note: *Materials and cutting listed will make two place mats.*

1. Cut one 12" by fabric width strip white/cream tonal; subcut strip into two 8" A rectangles. Trim the remainder into four 1½" x 10½" C strips and eight 1½" x 4½" E strips.

2. Cut one 22" by fabric width strip white/cream tonal; subcut strip into two 16" backing rectangles.

3. Cut one 2½" x 21" strip dark red/burgundy mottled; subcut strips into two 4½" D rectangles.

4. Cut one 4½" x 21" strip medium red/burgundy tonal; subcut strip into four 2½" F rectangles.

5. Cut two 2½" by fabric width strips burgundy mottled; subcut strip into six 10½" B strips.

6. Cut two 1½" by fabric width strips burgundy mottled; subcut strips into four 18½" G strips.

7. Cut four 2¼" by fabric width strips burgundy mottled for binding.

Bouquet in a Jar 1
6" x 10" Block
Make 1

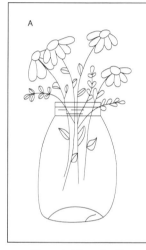

Bouquet in a Jar 2
6" x 10" Block
Make 1

Completing the Embroidered Blocks
1. Fold and crease each A rectangle to mark the vertical and horizontal centers.

2. Center and transfer the Bouquet in a Jar 1 and 2 embroidery designs on page 35 to the A rectangles referring to Redwork Basics on page 2.

3. Complete the redwork embroidery on the marked rectangles referring to Redwork Basics on page 2.

4. Trim the embroidered A rectangles to 6½" x 10½", centering the designs, to complete the Bouquet in a Jar blocks.

Completing the Place Mats
1. Select one Bouquet in a Jar block; one D rectangle; two each C, F and G strips; three B strips and four E strips for one place mat.

2. To complete one place mat, sew a B strip to opposite long sides of the Bouquet in a Jar block

and add C to the right long side as shown in Figure 1; press seams toward B strips.

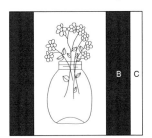

B **C**

Figure 1

3. Sew E to opposite long sides of D and add E to the top and bottom to complete the D-E unit as shown in Figure 2; press seams toward E strips.

E

E D

Figure 2

House of White Birches, Berne, Indiana 46711   Clotilde.com

4. Add F to the top and bottom of the D-E unit to complete the D-E-F unit referring to Figure 3; press seams toward F.

Figure 3

5. Sew the D-E-F unit to the B side of the previously pieced unit and add the third B strip and then the remaining C strip to the remaining long side of the D-E-F unit as shown in Figure 4; press seams toward B strips.

Figure 4

6. Sew a G strip to opposite long sides of the pieced unit referring to the Placement Diagram to complete one place mat top; press seams toward G strips.

7. Repeat all steps to complete a second place mat top.

8. Press each place mat top on both sides; check for proper seam pressing and trim all loose threads.

9. Sandwich one batting rectangle between one stitched top and a prepared backing rectangle; pin or baste layers together to hold. Quilt as desired by hand or machine. *Note: The sample place mats were machine-quilted in a meandering design using cream thread in the cream pieces and red thread in the red/ burgundy pieces.*

10. When quilting is complete, trim batting and backing fabric even with raw edges of each place mat top.

11. Join binding strips on short ends with diagonal seams to make one long strip as shown in Figure 5; trim seams to ¼" and press seams open.

Figure 5

12. Fold the binding strip with wrong sides together along length; press.

13. Sew binding to each place mat edge, mitering corners and overlapping ends. Fold binding to the back sides and stitch in place to finish the place mats. ❖

Bouquet in a Jar 1 Place Mat
Placement Diagram 18" x 12"

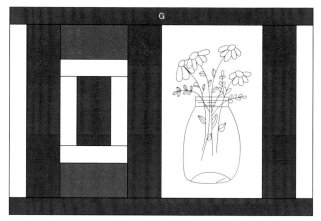

Bouquet in a Jar 2 Place Mat
Placement Diagram 18" x 12"

Note: *The number of leaves, stems and lines on the jar tops in the sample projects may vary slightly from the patterns given here.*

Bouquet Embroidery Design 1

Bouquet Embroidery Design 2

Bouquet in a Jar Table Runner

This charming table runner will bring back memories of picking a wildflower bouquet to place in Grandma's canning jar.

Project Specifications
Skill Level: Beginner
Runner Size: 39" x 16"
Block Size: 6" x 10" and 3" x 3"
Number of Blocks: 2 and 2

Materials
- 1 fat quarter dark red/burgundy tonal
- ½ yard red mottled
- ½ yard red tonal
- ½ yard white/cream tonal
- Batting 47" x 24"
- Backing 47" x 24"
- All-purpose thread to match fabrics
- Red and white quilting thread
- Red embroidery floss
- Large-eye embroidery needle
- Basic sewing tools and supplies

Cutting
1. Cut one 8" by fabric width strip white/cream tonal; subcut strip into two 12" A rectangles. Trim the remainder into four 1½" x 10½" D strips and four 3½" x 3½" E squares.

2. Cut two 1½" x 35½" I strips white/cream tonal.

3. Cut two 2½" x 21" strips dark red/burgundy tonal; subcut strips into four 10½" C strips.

4. Cut two 2½" x 12½" J strips dark red/burgundy tonal.

5. Cut one 3½" by fabric strip red mottled; subcut strip into two 1½" G strips and one 2½" H rectangle. Trim strip to 2½" and cut two 2½" x 10½" B strips.

6. Cut one 2½" by fabric width strip red mottled; subcut strip into two 10½" B strips.

7. Cut two 2½" x 39½" K strips red mottled.

8. Cut one 1½" by fabric width strip red tonal; subcut strip into eight 1½" F squares.

9. Cut four 2¼" by fabric width strips red tonal for binding.

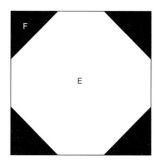

Snowball
3" x 3" Block
Make 2

Bouquet in a Jar 1
6" x 10" Block
Make 1

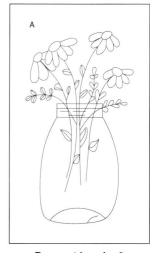

Bouquet in a Jar 2
6" x 10" Block
Make 1

Completing the Embroidered Blocks
1. Fold and crease each A rectangle to mark the vertical and horizontal centers.

2. Center and transfer the Bouquet in a Jar embroidery designs given on page 35 to the A rectangles referring to Redwork Basics on page 2.

3. Complete the redwork embroidery on the marked rectangles referring to Redwork Basics on page 2.

4. Trim the embroidered A rectangles to 6½" x 10½", centering the designs.

5. Sew a B strip to opposite long sides and C strips to the top and bottom of each of the embroidered A rectangles to complete the Bouquet in a Jar 1 and 2 blocks; press seams toward B and C strips.

Completing the Snowball Blocks

1. Mark a diagonal line from corner to corner on the wrong side of each F square.

2. Place a marked F square on each corner of an E square and stitch on the marked lines as shown in Figure 1.

Figure 1   **Figure 2**

3. Trim seams beyond the stitched line to ¼" and press F pieces to the right side to complete one Snowball block as shown in Figure 2.

4. Repeat steps 2 and 3 to complete a second Snowball block.

Completing the Table Runner

1. Join the two Snowball blocks with the H rectangle and add G strips to the ends as shown in Figure 3; press seams toward H and G.

Figure 3

2. Sew D strips to opposite sides of the pieced strip as shown in Figure 4; press seams toward D strips.

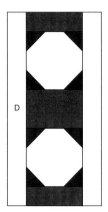

Figure 4

3. Sew a D strip to the bottom of each embroidered block and sew the block tops to the pieced strip as shown in Figure 5; press seams toward the embroidered blocks.

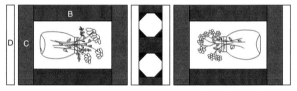

Figure 5

4. Sew I strips to opposite long sides of the pieced center; press seams toward I strips.

5. Sew J strips to opposite short ends and K strips to opposite long sides to complete the runner top; press seams toward J and K strips.

6. Press the runner top on both sides; check for proper seam pressing and trim all loose threads.

7. Sandwich the batting rectangle between the completed runner top and the prepared backing piece; pin or baste layers together to hold. Quilt as desired by hand or machine. ***Note:*** *The sample table runner was machine-quilted in a meandering design using cream thread in the cream pieces and red thread in the dark red/burgundy pieces.*

8. When quilting is complete, trim batting and backing fabric even with raw edges of the runner top.

9. Join binding strips on short ends with diagonal seams to make one long strip as shown in Figure 6; trim seams to ¼" and press seams open.

¼"

Figure 6

10. Fold the binding strip with wrong sides together along length; press.

11. Sew binding to the runner edges, mitering corners and overlapping ends. Fold binding to the back side and stitch in place to finish the table runner. ❖

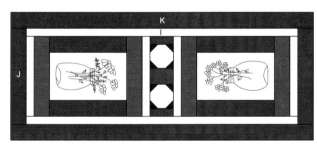

Bouquet in a Jar Table Runner
Placement Diagram 39" x 16"

Seed Packet Hand Towels

Your kitchen will sparkle and shine when you display these delightful embroidered towels. They are fun, fresh and functional!

Project Specifications
Skill Level: Beginner
Towel Size: Size Varies

Materials
- 7 cotton dish towels
- Red embroidery floss
- Large-eye embroidery needle
- Basic sewing tools and supplies

Completing the Redwork Embroidery
1. Fold and crease each dish towel on one diagonal to mark the center of one corner.

2. Trace one of the seed packet embroidery designs on a creased line approximately 3½" from the corner and 1½" from side edges using patterns given on pages 42–44, and referring to Figure 1 and the Redwork Basics on page 2.

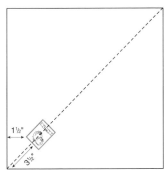

Figure 1

3. Complete the redwork embroidery on all marked pieces, referring to the Redwork Basics on page 2.

4. Remove transfer marks, if necessary, to complete the tea towels. ❖

Aster Seed Packet Embroidery Design

House of White Birches, Berne, Indiana 46711   Clotilde.com

Cosmos Seed Packet Embroidery Design

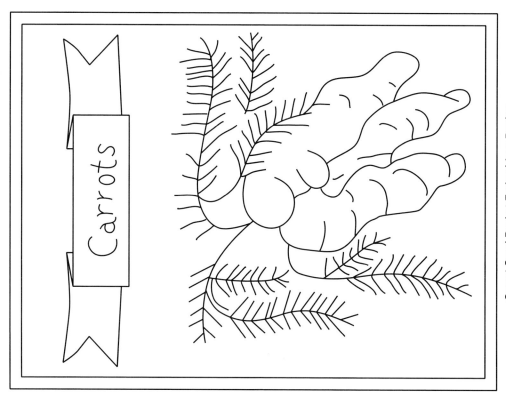

Carrot Seed Packet Embroidery Design

Pansy Seed Packet Embroidery Design

Daisy Seed Packet Embroidery Design

House of White Birches, Berne, Indiana 46711   Clotilde.com

Sweet Peas

Tomato

Sweet Peas Seed Packet Embroidery Design

Tomato Seed Packet Embroidery Design

Tomato Seed Packet Towel
Placement Diagram Size Varies

Sweet Peas Seed Packet Towel
Placement Diagram Size Varies

Carrot Seed Packet Towel
Placement Diagram Size Varies

Aster Seed Packet Towel
Placement Diagram Size Varies

House of White Birches, Berne, Indiana 46711   Clotilde.com

Daisy Seed Packet Towel
Placement Diagram Size Varies

Cosmos Seed Packet Towel
Placement Diagram Size Varies

Pansy Seed Packet Towel
Placement Diagram Size Varies

METRIC CONVERSION CHARTS

Metric Conversions

Canada/U.S. Measurement		Multiplied by		Metric Measurement
yards	x	.9144	=	metres (m)
yards	x	91.44	=	centimetres (cm)
inches	x	2.54	=	centimetres (cm)
inches	x	25.40	=	millimetres (mm)
inches	x	.0254	=	metres (m)

Canada/U.S. Measurement		Multiplied by		Metric Measurement
centimetres	x	.3937	=	inches
metres	x	1.0936	=	yards

Standard Equivalents

Canada/U.S. Measurement		Metric Measurement			Canada/U.S. Measurement		Metric Measurement		
⅛ inch	=	3.20 mm	=	0.32 cm	1⅜ yards	=	125.73 cm	=	1.26 m
¼ inch	=	6.35 mm	=	0.635 cm	1½ yards	=	137.16 cm	=	1.37 m
⅜ inch	=	9.50 mm	=	0.95 cm	1⅝ yards	=	148.59 cm	=	1.49 m
½ inch	=	12.70 mm	=	1.27 cm	1¾ yards	=	160.02 cm	=	1.60 m
⅝ inch	=	15.90 mm	=	1.59 cm	1⅞ yards	=	171.44 cm	=	1.71 m
¾ inch	=	19.10 mm	=	1.91 cm	2 yards	=	182.88 cm	=	1.83 m
⅞ inch	=	22.20 mm	=	2.22 cm	2⅛ yards	=	194.31 cm	=	1.94 m
1 inches	=	25.40 mm	=	2.54 cm	2¼ yards	=	205.74 cm	=	2.06 m
⅛ yard	=	11.43 cm	=	0.11 m	2⅜ yards	=	217.17 cm	=	2.17 m
¼ yard	=	22.86 cm	=	0.23 m	2½ yards	=	228.60 cm	=	2.29 m
⅜ yard	=	34.29 cm	=	0.34 m	2⅝ yards	=	240.03 cm	=	2.40 m
½ yard	=	45.72 cm	=	0.46 m	2¾ yards	=	251.46 cm	=	2.51 m
⅝ yard	=	57.15 cm	=	0.57 m	2⅞ yards	=	262.88 cm	=	2.63 m
¾ yard	=	68.58 cm	=	0.69 m	3 yards	=	274.32 cm	=	2.74 m
⅞ yard	=	80.00 cm	=	0.80 m	3⅛ yards	=	285.75 cm	=	2.86 m
1 yard	=	91.44 cm	=	0.91 m	3¼ yards	=	297.18 cm	=	2.97 m
1⅛ yards	=	102.87 cm	=	1.03 m	3⅜ yards	=	308.61 cm	=	3.09 m
1¼ yards	=	114.30 cm	=	1.14 m	3½ yards	=	320.04 cm	=	3.20 m
					3⅝ yards	=	331.47 cm	=	3.31 m
					3¾ yards	=	342.90 cm	=	3.43 m
					3⅞ yards	=	354.32 cm	=	3.54 m
					4 yards	=	365.76 cm	=	3.66 m
					4⅛ yards	=	377.19 cm	=	3.77 m
					4¼ yards	=	388.62 cm	=	3.89 m
					4⅜ yards	=	400.05 cm	=	4.00 m
					4½ yards	=	411.48 cm	=	4.11 m
					4⅝ yards	=	422.91 cm	=	4.23 m
					4¾ yards	=	434.34 cm	=	4.34 m
					4⅞ yards	=	445.76 cm	=	4.46 m
					5 yards	=	457.20 cm	=	4.57 m

Garden Party Stitchery is published by DRG, 306 East Parr Road, Berne, IN 46711. Printed in USA. Copyright © 2012 DRG. All rights reserved. This publication may not be reproduced in part or in whole without written permission from the publisher.

RETAIL STORES: If you would like to carry this pattern book or any other DRG publications, visit DRGwholesale.com

Every effort has been made to ensure that the instructions in this pattern book are complete and accurate. We cannot, however, take responsibility for human error, typographical mistakes or variations in individual work. Please visit ClotildeCustomerCare.com to check for pattern updates.

ISBN: 978-1-59217-367-9

1 2 3 4 5 6 7 8 9

HOUSE of
WHITE
BIRCHES
PUBLISHERS
SINCE 1947

Photo Index

10

5

13

28

36

41

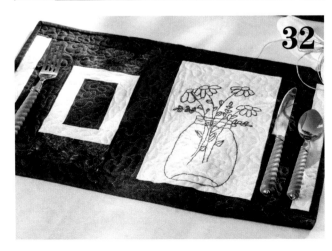

32